A Basic Latin Vocabulary

The First 1000 Words

J. Wilson & C. Parsons

Published by Bristol Classical Press
General Editor: John H. Betts

First published in 1960 by Macmillan Education Ltd.

Second edition published in 1992 by Thomas Nelson and Sons Ltd.

This edition published in 1996 by
Bristol Classical Press
an imprint of
Gerald Duckworth & Co. Ltd
The Old Piano Factory
48 Hoxton Square, London N1 6PB

A catalogue record for this book is available
from the British Library

ISBN 1-85399-505-3

Available in USA and Canada from:
Focus Information Group
PO Box 369
Newburyport
MA 01950

Printed in Great Britain by
Booksprint, Bristol

PREFACE

THIS selection includes a thousand of the most common Latin words and word-groups, as a basic vocabulary for first examinations.

Since many pupils tend to despair when faced with the simultaneous difficulties of grammar, syntax and vocabulary in translating a Latin author, it is hoped that by mastering ' The First 1000 Words ' they will gain not only a good working vocabulary, but also increased confidence.

We have tried to make the English meanings as real and significant as possible by grouping together Latin words which have a common root and connected meanings, by giving English derivations wherever possible, and by omitting English words or phrases which would be quite outside the experience of any pupil. A few marks of scansion are given to avoid ambiguity, e.g. *sŏlum* (ground), *sōlum* (only).

We have omitted from the alphabetical list:

(a) Prepositions and prefixes. A full list of these is given at the back of the book. Words whose meaning can be guessed by a simple addition of the prefix are not given in the alphabetical list: other compounded words are given. Thus the list contains *invenio* (find) but not *ineo* (go in).

(b) Numerals. These are also best learned by themselves, and a list of the most important numerals is given at the back.

(c) Some common conjunctions, which are best learnt in the context of syntax and construction. A summary of Latin constructions including these words is also given at the back.

We should like to thank The Rev. F. J. Shirley, D.D., Ph.D., and Mr. A. S. Mackintosh for their valuable assistance.

J. B. W.
A. C. P.

CONTENTS

VOCABULARY

A

abdo, -dere, -didi, -ditum	hide	
abhinc	ago	
absum, abesse, afui	be absent	absence
accĭdit, -cidere, -cĭdit	it happens	accident
accipio, -cipere, -cepi, *-ceptum*	receive, accept	accept
accuso (1)	accuse	accuse
acer, acris, acre	sharp, keen	acrid
acerbus, -a, -um	bitter	
acies, -iei, f.	battle-line	
⎰ *acuo, -cuere, -cui, -cutum*	sharpen	acute
⎱ *acutus, -a, -um*	sharp, pointed	
addo, -dere, -didi, -ditum	add	addition
adeo	to such an extent, so much	
adimo, -dimere, -demi, *-demptum*	take away	
adipiscor, adipisci, adeptus	obtain, acquire	
aditus, -us, m.	approach	
⎰ *adolesco, -lescere, -levi,* *adultum*	grow up	adult
⎱ *adolescens, -entis,* m.	young man	adolescent
adorior, adoriri, adortus	attack	
adsum, adesse, adfui	be present	
adventus, -us, m.	arrival	advent
adversus, -a, -um	facing, opposed	adverse

1

aedes, -ium, f. pl.	house	edifice
aedifico (1)	build	
aeger, -gra, -grum	ill, sick	
aegre	scarcely, with difficulty	
aemulor (1)	rival	emulate
aemulus, -a, -um (+dat.)	rivalling, jealous	
aequus, -a, -um	level, fair	equal
aequor, -oris, m.	sea, flat plain	
āēr, āĕris, m.	air	aeroplane
āēs, āēris, n.	copper, bronze	
aestas, -atis, f.	summer, heat	
aestimo (1)	value, reckon	estimate
aestus, -us, m.	heat, tide	estuary
aetas, -atis, f.	age	
aether, -eris, m.	air	ethereal
aevum, -i, n.	era, period of time	
✓ *ager, -gri*, m.	territory, field	agriculture
agrestis, -is, -e	of the country	
✓ *agricola, -ae*, m.	farmer	
agger, -eris, m.	rampart	
aggredior, -edi, -essus	approach, attack	aggression
✓ *agnosco, -oscere, -ovi, -itum*	recognise	
ago, agere, egi, actum	do, drive, carry on	agent
agmen, -minis, n.	army, marching-column	
ait	he says, he said	
ala, -ae, f.	wing	
alacer, -cris, -cre	brisk, quick	alacrity
✓ *albus, -a, -um*	white	albino
✓ *aliquis, -quis, -quid*	someone	

BASIC LATIN VOCABULARY

3

alius, -a, -ud	other, another	alias
alienus, -a, -um	belonging to another	alien
alter, -tera, -terum	the other, the second	alternate
altus, -a, -um	high, deep	altitude
ambulo (1)	walk	amble
amicus, -i, m.	friend	amicable
amicitia, -ae, f.	friendship	
amitto, -ittere, -isi, -issum	lose	
amo (1)	love, like	amorous
amor, -oris, m.	love, desire	
amplector, -ecti, -exus	embrace	
amplius	more, more fully	ample
anceps, (-cipitis)	doubtful	
angustus, -a, -um	narrow	
angustiae, -arum, f. pl.	narrow pass, defile	
animadverto, -ertere, -erti, -ersum	notice	
anima, -ae, f.	spirit, life, breath	animal
animus, -i, m.	mind, courage	animosity
annus, -i, m.	year	annual
ante	before (preposition)	antecedent
antea	before (adverb)	
antequam	before (conjunction)	
antrum, -i, n.	cave	
aperio, -perire, -perui, -pertum	open (trans.)	aperture
appareo (2)	appear, be visible	apparent
appello (1)	call	appeal
appropinquo (1) (+dat.)	approach	
aptus, -a, -um	suitable, appropriate	apt

✓ *aqua, -ae*, f.	water	aqueduct
✓ *aquila, -ae*, f.	eagle, battle-flag	
āra, -ae, f.	altar	
{ *ăro* (1)	plough	arable
{ *ăratrum, -i*, n.	plough	
{ *arvum, -i*, n.	field	
arbitror (1)	think	arbitrate
arbor, -oris, f.	tree	
arceo (2)	ward off, keep away	
arcesso, -ssere, -ssivi, -ssitum	send for	
✓ *arcus, -us*, m.	bow (weapon), arch	arch
ardeo, ardere, arsi, arsum	burn (intrans.)	ardent
arduus, -a, -um	steep, towering, difficult	arduous
✓ *argentum, -i*, n.	silver, money	
arguo, -uere, -ui, -utum	prove, accuse	argue
✓ *aridus, -a, -um*	dry	arid
{ *arma, -orum*, n. pl.	weapons, arms	armoury
{ *armo* (1)	arm	
✓ *ars, artis*, f.	skill, art	artistic
artus, -um, m. pl.	limbs	articulate
arx, arcis, f.	citadel, fortress	
ascendo, -endere, -endi, -ensum	climb	ascend
asper, -era, -erum	rough	asperity
✓ *astrum, -i*, n.	star	astronomy
at	but	
✓ *atque, ac*	and	
{ *auctor, -oris*, m. or f.	person responsible for	author
{ *auctoritas, -atis*, f.	authority, influence	authority
{ *audeo, audere, ausu°*	dare	
{ *audax (-acis)*	daring, bold, rash	audacious
{ *audacia, -ae*, f.	boldness, rashness	

BASIC LATIN VOCABULARY

audio (4)	hear	audience
augeo, augere, auxi, auctum	increase (trans.)	auction
aura, -ae, f.	breeze, air	
aurum, -i, n.	gold	
aut	either, or	
autem	moreover, but	
auxilium, -i, n.	help (in plural, auxiliary troops)	auxiliary
avidus, -a, -um	greedy, desirous	avid
avus, -i, m.	grandfather, ancestor	

B

barbarus, -a, -um	foreign, barbarous	barbarians
bellum, -i, n.	war	rebellion
benignus, -a, -um	kind	benign
bibo, -bere, -bi, -bitum	drink	imbibe
blandus, -a, -um	nice, pleasant	bland
blandior (4) (+dat.)	flatter	
bonus, -a, -um	good	bonny
bonum, -i, n.	advantage (in plural: goods, possessions)	
bene	well	beneficial
bos, bovis, m.	ox	bovine
bracchium, -i, n.	arm (of body)	bracelet
brevis, -is, -e	short	brevity

C

cadaver, -eris, n.	corpse	cadaverous
cădo, cadere, cecĭdi, cāsum	fall	
cāsus, -us, m.	fall, occurrence, chance	case
caecus, -a, -um	blind	

caedo, caedere, cecĭdi, caesum	cut, beat, kill	incision
caedes, -is, f.	murder, slaughter	
✓ *caelum, -i,* n.	sky, heaven, climate	
caelestis, -is, -e	of the sky, heavenly	celestial
✓ *calidus, -a, -um*	warm, hot	
callidus, -a, -um	clever, cunning	
✓ *campus, -i,* m.	plain, field	
candidus, -a, -um	white, bright	candid
✓ *canis, -is,* m.	dog	canine
cano, canere, cecini, cantum	sing	
canto (1)	sing	chant
✓ *carmen, -minis,* n.	song, poem (in plural, poetry)	
capio, capere, cepi, captum	take, get, contain	capture
✓ *captivus, -i,* m.	prisoner	captive
✓ *caput, -pitis,* n.	head	capital
carcer, -ceris, m.	prison	incarcerate
căreo, carere, carui, caritum (+abl.)	be without, lack	
carpo, -pere, -psi, -ptum	pluck, use, slander	carp
✓ *cārus, -a, -um*	dear	
castra, -orum, n. pl.	camp	
✓ *castellum, -i,* n.	fort	castle
✓ *căveo, cavere, cāvi, cautum*	take care, beware	caution
cavus, -a, -um	hollow	cave
cedo, cedere, cessi, cessum	go, yield	procession
celeber, -bris, -bre	famous, crowded	celebrated
celer, -leris, -lere	swift	celerity
celo (1)	hide	conceal
✓ *cena, -ae,* f.	dinner	
censeo, -sere, -sui, -sum	think, vote, value	censor
✓ *centurio, -ionis,* m.	centurion	centurion

cerno, cernere, crevi, cretum	see, distinguish	discern
{ *certo* (1)	fight, struggle	concert
{ *certamen, -minis,* n.	struggle	
certus, -a, -um	sure, fixed	certain
cervix, -vicis, f.	neck	cervical
cesso (1)	delay, be slow, stop	cease
ceterus, -a, -um	remaining, the rest	etcetera
cibus, -i, m.	food	
{ *cieo, ciere, civi, citum*	rouse, summon, stir up	excite
{ *cito* (1)	rouse, summon, stir up	
{ *cito*	quickly	
cingo, cingere, cinxi, cinctum	surround	precinct
cinis, cineris, m.	ashes	incinerate
circumdo, -dare, -dedi, -datum	surround	
{ *citra*	on this side of	
{ *citerior (citerioris)*	nearer	
{ *civis, -is,* m. or f.	citizen	civilian
{ *civilis, -is, -e*	civil, of citizens	civil
{ *civitas, -atis,* f.	state, country	
clades, -is, f.	defeat, disaster	
{ *clamo* (1)	shout	clamour
{ *clamor, -oris,* m.	shout	
clarus, -a, -um	famous, clear	clarity
classis, -is, f.	fleet	
claudo, claudere, clausi, clausum	shut	conclude
coepi (fut. coepero, past coeperam)	began	

coerceo (2)	confine, control	coerce
cogito (1)	think, ponder	cogitate
cognosco, -noscere, -novi, -nitum	find out, get to know	recognise
cogo, cogere, coegi, coactum	compel, drive, collect (trans.)	cogent
cohors, cohortis, f.	cohort, band of troops	cohort
cohortor (1)	encourage	
collis, -is, m.	hill	
collum, -i, n.	neck	collar
colo, colere, colui, cultum	cultivate, worship, pay attention to	culture
color, -oris, m.	colour	colour
coma, -ae, f.	hair, leaves of trees	
comes, comitis, m. or f.	companion	
commeatus, -us, m.	supplies, provisions	
comminus	at close quarters	
committo, -mittere, -misi, -missum	join, commit, entrust	commit
commodus, -a, -um	convenient, advantageous	
commodum, -i, n.	advantage, profit	commodity
comparo (1)	procure, obtain	
comperio, -perire, -perui, pertum	find out, discover	
compleo, -plere, -plevi, -pletum	fill up	complement
complures, -es, -a	several, a fair number of	
comprehendo, -endere, -endi, -ensum	seize, understand	comprehend
concido, -cidere, -cidi	fall, collapse	
concido, -cidere, -cidi, -cisum	cut down, destroy	concise

concilio (1)	win over, conciliate	reconcile
concilium, -i, n.	association, council	council
condo, -dere, -didi, -ditum	establish, store, bury	
conficio, -ficere, -feci, *-fectum*	finish, do, make	confectionery
confectus, -a, -um	exhausted	
coniunx, -iugis, m. or f.	husband, wife	conjugal
coniuro (1)	swear, conspire	conjure
coniuratus, -i, m.	conspirator	
conor (1)	try	
consentio, -entire, -ensi, *-ensum*	agree	consent
consilium, -i, n.	plan, policy	counsel
consisto, -sistere, -stiti, *-stitum*	stand still, stop	consistent
conspicio, -spicere, -spexi, *-spectum*	perceive	
conspicuus, -a, -um	visible, outstanding	conspicuous
conspectus, -us, m.	sight, view	
constans (constantis)	brave, resolute	constant
constantia, -ae, f.	bravery	
constat, -stare, -stitit	it is agreed	
constituo, -uere, -ui, -utum	decide, establish	constitution
consuesco, -suescere, -suevi, *-suetum*	accustom, be accustomed	
consuetudo, -dinis, f.	custom, habit	
consulo, -sulere, -sului, *-sultum*	consult	consult
consul, -ulis, m.	consul	
contemno, -temnere, -tempsi, *-temptum*	despise	contempt

contendo, -tendere, -tendi, -tentum	march, strive, hasten	contend
contineo, -tinere, -tinui, -tentum	keep in, enclose	contain
contio, -ionis, f.	meeting, assembly	
{ *copia, -ae,* f.	abundance, supply	copious
{ *copiae, -arum,* f. pl.	troops, forces	
✓ *cor, cordis,* n.	heart	cordial
cornu, -us, n.	horn, wing (of an army)	
✓ *corpus, -poris,* n.	body	corporal
{ *cotidie*	daily	
{ *cotidianus, -a, -um*	daily	
✓ { *cras*	tomorrow	procrastinate
{ *crastinus, -a, -um*	of tomorrow	
{ *creber, -bra, -brum*	numerous, frequent	
{ *crebro*	frequently	
✓ *credo, -dere, -didi, -ditum* (+dat.)	believe, entrust	credulous
creo (1)	make, create	creation
cresco, crescere, crevi, cretum	grow (intrans.)	
crimen, -minis, n.	accusation, crime	criminal
✓ *crudelis, -is, -e*	cruel	
✓ *crus, cruris,* n.	leg	
cubo, cubare, cubui, cubitum	lie down	
✓ { *culpa, -ae,* f.	blame	culpable
{ *culpo* (1)	blame	
cum	when, since, although	
cunctus, -a, -um	all	

cunctor (1)	delay, go slowly	
cupio, cupere, cupivi, cupitum	desire	
cupidus, -a, -um	eager, desirous	cupidity
cupido, -dinis, f.	desire, passion, love	cupid
cur	why	
cura, -ae, f.	care, anxiety	curate
curo (1)	care for, look after	
curia, -ae, f.	senate-house	
curro, currere, cucurri, cursum	run	current
currus, -us, m.	chariot	
cursus, -us, m.	running, course	
custos, -todis, m.	guard, guardian	custodian
custodio (4)	guard	

D

damno (1)	condemn	damnation
damnum, -i, n.	loss, damage	
daps, dapis, f.	feast, banquet	
dea, -ae, f.	gooddess	
deus, -i, m.	god	deify
debeo (2)	owe, ought, have to	debit
decerno, -cernere, -crevi, -cretum	decide, decree	
decet, -ere, -uit	it is fitting	decent
dedecet, -ere, -uit	it is disgraceful	
decus, decoris, n.	honour, beauty, glory	
dedecus, dedecoris, n.	disgrace, dishonour	
decorus, -a, -um	honourable, handsome	
declaro (1)	state, declare	declare

dedo, -dere, -didi, -ditum	surrender (trans.)	
deditio, -ionis, f.	surrender	
defendo, -dere, -di, -sum	defend	defence
deficio, -ficere, -feci, *-fectum*	be disloyal, fail, run short	deficient
deinde	then, next	
deleo, -lere, -levi, -letum	destroy	delete
deligo, -ligere, -legi, -lectum	choose out, select	
demens (-entis)	mad	demented
demo, demere, dempsi, *demptum*	take away	
demum	finally, certainly	
denique	finally, to end with	
descendo, -endere, -endi, *-ensum*	go down	descend
desidero (1)	long for	
desiderium, -i, n.	desire, longing	desire
desino, -sinere, -sii, *-situm*	leave off, cease	
desisto, -sistere, -stiti, *-stitum*	leave off, cease	desist
despero (1)	despair	desperate
desum, deesse, defui	not to be there, be lacking	
deterreo (2)	frighten away, deter	deter
detrimentum, -i, n.	loss, damage	detriment
dexter, -tra, -trum or *-tera,* *-terum*	right (direction)	dexterity
dextrā (manu)	on the right (hand)	
dico, dicere, dixi, dictum	say, speak	dictionary
dies, diei, m. or f.	day	
difficilis, -is, -e	difficult	difficulty
digitus, -i, m.	finger	digit

dignus, -a, -um (+abl.)	worthy of	
dignitas, -atis, f.	worth, dignity	dignity
diligo, -ligere, -lexi, -lectum	love	
diligentia, -ae, f.	diligence, care	diligent
dimico (1)	fight	
dimidius, -a, -um	half	
dimidium, -i, n.	a half	
dirus, -a, -um	dreadful, fearful	dire
disco, discere, didici	learn	disciple
discors, -cordis	disagreeing	discordant
discrimen, -minis, n.	crisis, difference	discriminate
dissimilis, -is, -e (+gen.)	unlike	dissimilar
dissimulo (1)	pretend not to, conceal	dissimulate
diu	for a long time	
divido, -videre, -visi, -visum	divide	division
do, dăre, dedi, datum	give	data
dono (1)	give	donation
donum, -i, n.	gift	
doceo, -cere, -cui, -ctum	teach	doctrine
doleo, -lere, -lui, -litum	suffer pain, grieve for	dolour
dolor, -oris, m.	pain, grief	
dolus, -i, m.	trick, cunning	
domo, domare, domui, domitum	tame, conquer	
dominus, -i, m.	lord, master	dominate
domus, -us, f.	house, home	domicile
donec	until	
dubius, -a, -um	doubtful	dubious
dubium, -i, n.	doubt	
dubito (1)	doubt	

✓ duco, ducere, duxi, ductum	lead	conduct
dux, ducis, m.	leader, commander	duke
✓ dulcis, -is, -e	sweet, pleasant	dulcet
duplex (duplicis)	double	duplicate
durus, -a, -um	hard	durable
duro (1)	last, make hard	endure

E

✓ ecce!	look!	
en!	look!	
ĕdo, esse, ēdi, ēsum	eat	
efficio, -ficere, -feci, -fectum	cause, perform, do	effect
egeo, egere, egui (+abl.)	need, want, lack	
✓ ego (mei)	I	egoist
egredior, -gredi, -gressus (+abl.)	go out, disembark	
egregius, -a, -um	uncommon, excellent	
eminus	at a distance	
ĕmo, emere, ēmi, emptum	buy	redeem
✓ enim	for	
ensis, -is, m.	sword	
eo, ire, ivi (or ii), itum	go	exit
eo	to there	
epistula, -ae, f.	letter, epistle	epistle
✓ equus, -i, m.	horse	
eques, equitis, m.	horseman	
equitatus, -us, m.	cavalry	
equester, -tris, -tre	of cavalry, mounted	equestrian
✓ ergo	therefore	

erro (1)	go wrong, wander	err
{ *erumpo, -umpere, -upi,* *-uptum*	break out, sally forth	erupt
{ *eruptio, -ionis,* f.	sally, sortie	eruption
{ *et*	and	
{ *etiam*	also, even	
etsi	although, even if	
evenio, -nire, -ni, -ntum	happen, result	event
excelsus, -a, -um	high	
exemplum, -i, n.	example	example
{ *exerceo, -cere, -cui, -citum*	train, practise	exercise
{ *exercitus, -us,* m.	army	
exiguus, -a, -um	small, scanty	
exilium, -i, n.	exile, banishment	exile
eximius, -a, -um	special, excellent	
existimo (1)	value, think	
exitium, -i, n.	destruction	
expedio, -pedire, -pedivi, *-peditum*	prepare, equip, make easy	expedition
{ *experior, -periri, -pertus*	try, experience	expert
{ *experientia, -ae,* f.	experience	
expers (expertis) (+gen.)	having no part in	
explorator, -oris, m.	scout, spy	explorer
expugno (1)	take by assault, storm	
exspecto (1)	await, expect	expect
{ *extra*	outside	
{ *exterior (exterioris)*	on the outside	exterior
{ *extremus, -a, -um*	at the end, last	extreme

F

fabula, -ae, f.	story, tale	fabulous
facies, -iei, f.	face, appearance	face

facio, facere, feci, factum	do, make	fact
facinus, -noris, n.	deed, crime	
facilis, -is, -e	easy	facility
facultas, -atis, f.	means, opportunity	faculty
fallo, fallere, fefelli, falsum	deceive	fallacy
falsus, -a, -um	false	false
fallax (fallacis)	treacherous, deceitful	
fāma, -ae, f.	news, rumour, reputation	fame
fămes, famis, f.	hunger	famine
familia, -ae, f.	household, family	family
fas (indeclinable)	right, morality	
fateor, fateri, fassus	admit, confess	confess
fatigo (1)	tire, weary	fatigue
fatum, -i, n.	destiny, fate	fate
faveo, favere, favi, fautum (+dat.)	favour	favourite
felix (felicis)	fortunate, happy	felicity
femina, -ae, f.	woman	feminine
fere	almost, about	
fero, ferre, tuli, latum	carry, bring, bear, endure	refer
ferrum, -i, n.	iron weapon, sword	
ferreus, -a, -um	made of iron, cruel	
ferus, -a, -um	fierce, wild	
ferox (ferocis)	bold, savage, fierce	ferocious
fera, -ae, f.	wild animal	
fessus, -a, -um	tired, weary	
festino (1)	hasten, hurry	
fido, fidere, fisus (+dat.)	trust	confident
fides, -ei, f.	confidence, faith, loyalty	
fidelis, -is, -e	faithful	fidelity
figo, figere, fixi, fixum	**fix**	**fix**

filius, -i, m.	son	**filial**
filia, -ae, f.	daughter	
findo, findere, fidi, fissum	split	**fission**
fingo, fingere, finxi, fictum	make up, pretend	**fiction**
finis, -is, m.	end, limit	**final**
fines, -ium, m. pl.	territory, boundaries	
fio, fieri	become, be made	
firmo (1)	strengthen	**confirm**
firmus, -a, -um	firm, strong	**firm**
flagito (1)	demand, insist on	
flecto, flectere, flexi, flexum	bend (trans.)	**flexible**
fleo, flere, flevi, fletum	weep	
fletus, -us, m.	weeping	
flos, floris, m.	flower	**floral**
fluo, fluere, fluxi, fluxum	flow	**fluent**
fluctus, -us, m.	wave	**fluctuate**
flumen, -minis, n.	river	
fluvius, -i, m.	river	
fodio, fodere, fodi, fossum	dig	
fossa, -ae, f.	ditch, trench	**fosse**
foedus, foederis, n.	treaty	**federal**
foedus, -a, -um	foul	
fons, fontis, m.	fountain, spring, source	**fountain**
foris, -is, f.	door	
foris	out of doors, outside	
forma, -ae, f.	shape, beauty	**form**
formosus, -a, -um	beautiful	
fortis, -is, -e	brave, strong	**fort**
fortitudo, -dinis, f.	bravery	**fortitude**

forte	by chance	
fortuna, -ae, f.	fortune, fate	fortune
forsitan	perhaps	
fortasse	perhaps	
forum, -i, n.	market-place, forum	forum
frango, frangere, fregi, fractum	break (trans.)	fraction
frater, -tris, m.	brother	fraternal
fraus, fraudis, f.	trickery, deceit	fraud
frĕtum, -i, n.	strait, sea	
frētus, -a, -um (+abl.)	relying on	
frigus, -goris, n.	cold	refrigerator
frigidus, -a, -um	cold	frigid
fruges, -um, f. pl.	fruit, crops	
frumentum, -i, n.	corn	
frumentarius, -a, -um	of corn	
fruor, frui, fructus (+abl.)	enjoy	
frustra	in vain	frustrate
fugio, fugere, fugi, fugitum	flee, escape	fugitive
fuga, -ae, f.	flight	
fugo (1)	make to flee, rout	
fundo, fundere, fudi, fusum	pour, scatter, rout	refund
fungor, fungi, functus (+abl.)	perform, do	function
fur, furis, m.	thief	furtive
furor, -oris, m.	rage, madness	fury

G

gaudeo, gaudere, gavisus	rejoice, be glad	gaudy
gaudium, -i, n.	joy	

gemo, gemere, gemui, gemitum	make a noise, groan	
gemitus, -us, m.	noise, groan	
genus, generis, n.	race, kind, sort	general
gens, gentis, f.	tribe, people	gentile
gigno, gignere, genui, genitum	produce, give birth to	regenerate
✓ *genu, -us*, n.	knee	
gero, gerere, gessi, gestum	make, carry on, conduct	gesture
✓ *gladius, -i*, m.	sword	gladiator
glorior (1)	boast	
gloria, -ae, f.	glory	glory
gratus, -a, -um	pleasant, grateful	grateful
gratia, -ae, f.	charm, favour, thanks	grace
gravis, -is, -e	heavy, severe	grave
guberno (1)	steer, govern	govern
gubernator, -oris, m.	helmsman, director	governor
grex, gregis, f.	flock	segregate

H

✓ *habeo* (2)	have, hold	habit
haereo, haerere, haesi, haesum	stick	adhere
harena, -ae, f. (or *arena*)	sand	arena
hasta, -ae, f.	spear	
haud	not	
heres, heredis, m. or f.	heir, heiress	hereditary
heri	yesterday	
hesternus, -a, -um	of yesterday	

hic, haec, hoc	this	
hic	here	
huc	to here	
hinc	from here	
hiems, hiemis, f.	winter	
hiemo (1)	spend the winter	
hiberna, -orum, n. pl.	winter-camp, place to spend the winter	hibernate
hodie	today	
hodiernus, -a, -um	of today	
homo, hominis, m.	man, human being	homicide
humanus, -a, -um	human, humane, kind	humanity
honos, honoris, m.	honour, mark of honour	honour
honestus, -a, -um	honourable, noble	
hora, -ae, f.	hour	horoscope
horreo, horrere, horrui	fear, shrink from	
horror, -oris, m.	fear, trembling	horror
hortor (1)	encourage	exhort
hortus, -i, m.	garden	horticulture
hospes, hospitis, m.	host, guest stranger	hospitality
hostia, -ae, f.	victim, sacrifice	
hostis, -is, m. or f.	enemy	hostile
humus, -i, f.	ground, earth	
humilis, -is, -e	humble, low down	humility

I (vowel)

ibi	there
ictus, -us, m.	blow, stroke
idem, eadem, idem	the same
idoneus, -a, -um	suitable
igitur	therefore

ignarus, -a, -um	not knowing, ignorant	
ignoro (1)	not to know	ignorant
ignotus, -a, -um	unknown	
ignavus, -a, -um	cowardly, lazy	
ignis, -is, m.	fire	ignite
ignosco, -noscere, -novi, -notum (+dat.)	pardon, forgive	
ille, illa, illud	that	
illic	there	
illuc	to there	
illinc	from there	
illustris, -is, -e	famous, outstanding	illustrious
imago, imaginis, f.	image, appearance, picture	imagine
imber, imbris, m.	rain	
immanis, -is, -e	enormous, savage	
impedio (4)	hinder	
impedimentum, -i, n.	obstacle, hindrance	impediment
impedimenta, -orum, n. pl.	baggage	
impero (1) (+dat.)	order	imperious
imperium, -i, n.	command, power, empire	imperial
imperator, -oris, m.	general	
impetus, -us, m.	charge, attack	impetuous
impiger, -gra, -grum	active, energetic	
improbus, -a, -um	wicked, shameless	
inanis, -is, -e	empty	inane
incendo, -cendere, -cendi, -censum	burn (trans.)	
incendium, -i, n.	blaze, fire	incendiary
incertus, -a, -um	uncertain	
incipio, -cipere, -cepi, -ceptum	begin	

incola, -ae, m. or f.	inhabitant	
incolo (1)	inhabit	
incolumis, -is, -e	safe, unharmed	
incommodus, -a, -um	disadvantageous, awkward	
incommodum, -i, n.	disadvantage	
inde	from there, then	
induo, -duere, -dui, -dutum	put on	
indutiae, -arum, f. pl.	truce, armistice	
inermis, -is, -e	unarmed	
iners (inertis)	inactive	inert
infestus, -a, -um	hostile, dangerous	infested
infra	below	
inferior (inferioris)	lower	inferior
infimus, -a, -um or *imus, -a, -um*	lowest, bottom	
ingenium, -i, n.	mind, intellect, talent	ingenious
ingens (ingentis)	huge, big	
ingratus, -a, -um	unpleasant, ungrateful	ingratitude
iniquus, -a, -um	unjust, unequal, uneven	iniquity
initium, -i, n.	beginning	initiative
inopia, -ae, f.	poverty, need, shortage	
inopinatus, -a, -um	unexpected	
inquit	he says, he said	
inscius, -a, -um	not knowing	
insidior (1) (+dat.)	ambush, plot	insidious
insidiae, -arum, f. pl.	ambush, plot, treachery	
insignis, -is, -e	distinguished, outstanding	ensign
instruo, -uere, -uxi, -uctum	construct, arrange	instruct
insula, -ae, f.	island	insular
integer, -gra, -grum	untouched, fresh	integrity
intellego, -llegere, -llexi, -llectum	perceive, understand	intellect

intercludo, -udere, -usi, -usum	shut off, cut off	
interdum	sometimes	
✓ *interea*	meanwhile	
✓ *interim*	meanwhile	
intereo, -ire, -ii, -itum	die	
interest, -esse, -fuit (meā, tuā, etc.)	it concerns, it interests	interest
✓ *interficio, -ficere, -feci, -fectum*	kill	
✓ *intra*	within	
interior (interioris)	inner	interior
intimus, -a, -um	inmost	intimate
.intro (1)	enter	entrance
inutilis, -is, -e	useless	
✓ *invenio, -venire, -veni, -ventum*	find	invent
invideo, -videre, -vidi, -visum (+dat.)	envy, grudge	invidious
invidia, -ae, f.	jealousy	
invitus, -a, -um	unwilling	
ipse, ipsa, ipsum	(in nominative) self: (other cases) he, she, it	
ira, -ae, f.	anger	
irascor, irasci, iratus (+dat.)	be angry	
✓ *iratus, -a, -um*	angry	irate
is, ea, id	that: he, she, it	
iste, ista, istud	that: he, she, it	
ita	so, thus	
itaque	and so, therefore	
item	similarly, also	

iter, itineris, n.	journey, route	itinerary
iterum	again, a second time	reiterate

I (*consonant*)

iaceo (2)	lie down, lie	adjacent
iacio, iacere, ieci, iactum	throw	inject
iacto (1)	throw	
iaculum, -i, n.	javelin	
iam	now, already	
iubeo, iubere, iussi, iussum	order, command	
ius, iuris, n.	law, right	jury
iustus, -a, -um	just, right	just
iudex, iudicis, m.	judge, juryman	judicial
iudico (1)	judge	prejudice
iudicium, -i, n.	judgment	
iungo, -ere, iunxi, iunctum	join, yoke	junction
iugum, -i, n.	yoke, mountain ridge	
iuro (1)	swear	perjury
iuvenis, -is, m.	young man	juvenile
iuvo, iuvare, iuvi, iutum	help	

L

lābor, labi, lapsus	slip, fall, glide	lapse
lăbor, -oris, m.	work, toil	laboratory
lăboro (1)	work, be in difficulty	
lacer, -era, -erum	torn, mangled	lacerated
lacesso, -essere, -essivi, -essitum	provoke	
lacrimo (1)	weep	
lacrimae, -arum, f. pl.	tears	
laedo, laedere, laesi, laesum	hurt, damage	collision

✓ *laetus, -a, -um*	glad, happy	
laevus, -a, -um	left, on the left	
languidus, -a, -um	tired, weak	languid
lapis, -idis, m.	stone	
lassus, -a, -um	tired, weary	lassitude
{ *lateo, -tere, -tui*	be hidden, lurk	latent
{ *latebrae, -arum*, f. pl.	lair, hiding-place	
latro, -onis, m.	robber, brigand	
lătus, lateris, n.	side, flank	lateral
lātus, -a, -um	broad, wide	latitude
✓ { *laudo* (1)	praise	laud
{ *laus, laudis*, f.	praise	
lĕgo, legere, lēgi, lēctum	choose, read, collect	lecture
lēgatus, -i, m.	officer, representative	legation
✓ *lĕgio, -ionis*, f.	legion	legionary
lenis, -is, -e	mild, gentle	lenient
✓ *lentus, -a, -um*	slow	
✓ *leo, leonis*, m.	lion	leonine
{ *lĕvis, -is, -e*	light, easy	levity
{ *levo* (1)	lift, relieve	
✓ *lex, lēgis*, f.	law, statute	legal
✓ *lĭber, -bri*, m.	book	library
✓ { *līber, -era, -erum*	free	liberal
✓ { *lībero* (1)	free	liberate
{ *libertas, -atis*, f.	freedom	liberty
{ *libido, libidinis*, f.	desire, lust	
{ *libet, -bere, -buit* (+dat.)	it pleases	
līberi, -orum, m. pl.	children	
licet, -cere, -cuit (+dat.)	it is allowed	licence
lignum, -i, n.	wood	
ligo (1)	bind, tie	ligament
✓ *lingua, -ae*, f.	tongue, language	linguist

littera, -ae, f.	letter (of the alphabet)	literal
litterae, -arum, f. pl.	letter, epistle	
litus, litoris, n.	shore, coast	
loco (1)	place	locate
locus, -i, m.	place	local
longus, -a, -um	long	longitnde
longinquus, -a, -um	long, distant	
loquor, loqui, locutus	speak	soliloquy
ludo, ludere, lusi, lusum	play	ludicrous
lux, lucis, f.	light	
lumen, -minis, n.	light	luminous
luceo, lucere, luxi	shine, be bright	
lucidus, -a, -um	bright, clear	lucid
luna, -ae, f.	moon	lunar

M

maestus, -a, -um	sad	
magnus, -a, -um	great, large	magnate
magnopere	greatly	
magnitudo, -dinis, f.	greatness, size	magnitude
mālo, malle, malui	prefer	
mălus, -a, -um	bad	malice
mando (1)	order, entrust	mandate
māne	in the morning	
măneo, manere, mansi, mansum	stay, remain	mansion
mānes, -ium, m. pl.	ghosts, spirits of the dead	
mănus, -us, f.	hand, group of people	manual
mare, -ris, n.	sea	marine
mater, -tris, f.	mother	maternal
materia, -ae, f.	matter, material	material

maturo (1)	hurry, hasten	
maturus, -a, -um	ripe, mature	maturity
meditor (1)	think, meditate	meditate
medius, -a, -um	in the middle	mediaeval
mediocris, -is, -e	moderate	mediocre
membra, membrorum, n. pl.	limbs	member
memini (+fut. *-nero:* past. *-neram*) (+gen.)	remember	memento
memor (*memoris*) (+gen.)	remembering, mindful	
memoria, -ae, f.	memory	memorial
mens, mentis, f.	mind	mental
mensa, -ae, f.	table	
mensis, -is, m.	month	
mentior (4)	tell a lie	
merces, -cedis, f.	pay, price	mercenary
mercator, -oris, m.	trader, merchant	merchant
mereo (2) or *mereor* (2)	earn, deserve	merit
merito	deservedly	
meridies, -iei, m.	mid-day, south	meridian
metuo, -uere, -ui, -utun	fear	
metus, -us, m.	fear	
miles, militis, m.	soldier	
militaris, -is, -e	military	military
minor (1) (+dat.)	threaten	
minae, -arum, f. pl.	threats	
minuo, -uere, -ui, -utum	lessen, make smaller	minute
miror (1)	wonder at, admire	admire
mirus, -a, -um	wonderful	miracle
misceo, miscere, miscui, mixtum	mix, mingle, confuse (trans.)	mixture

miser, -era, -erum	wretched, miserable	miserable
misereor (2) (+gen.)	pity	
miseret, -ere, -uit (+ acc. and gen.)	it causes pity	
mitto, mittere, misi, missum	send	mission
mobilis, -is, -e	changeable	mobile
modus, -i, m.	way, manner	mode
modo	only, now, just now	
moenia, -ium, n. pl.	town walls, fortifications	
moles, -is, f.	mass, pile, bulk	
molior (4)	strive, plot, work hard at	demolish
mollis, -is, -e	soft	mollify
moneo (2)	warn	admonish
mons, montis, m.	mountain	mountain
monstro (1)	show	demonstrate
morbus, -i, m.	disease	morbid
mordeo, mordere, momordi, morsum	bite	
morsus, -us, m.	bite	
morior, mori, mortuus	die	
mors, mortis, f.	death	
mortalis, -is, -e	mortal, human	mortal
moror (1)	delay, check	
mora, -ae, f.	delay	
mos, moris, m.	custom, tradition	moral
moveo, movere, movi, motum	move (trans.)	move
mox	soon	
mulier, -ieris, f.	woman	
multus, -a, -um	many	multiply
multitudo, -dinis, f.	a great number, crowd	multitude
mundus, -i, m.	universe, world	mundane

munio (4)	fortify	
munitio, -ionis, f.	fortification	munitions
munus, muneris, n.	gift, job, public service	munificent
murus, -i, m.	wall	mural
muto (1)	change (trans.)	

N

nam	for	
nanciscor, nancisci, nactus (or *nanctus*)	get, obtain	
narro (1)	relate, tell	narrate
nascor, nasci, natus	be born	natal
natus, -i, m.	son	
natura, -ae, f.	nature	natural
natio, -ionis, f.	tribe, nation	national
navis, -is, f.	ship	navy
navigo (1)	sail	navigate
navigium, -i, n.	sailing, ship	
navalis, -is, -e	naval	naval
nauta, -ae, m.	sailor	nautical
nec, neque	neither, nor, and not	
necessarius, -a, -um	necessary, inevitable	necessary
neco (1)	kill	
nefas (indeclinable)	wrong, wickedness	
nefandus, -a, -um	wicked	
nefarius, -a, -um	wicked	nefarious
nego (1)	deny	negative
neglego, -legere, -lexi, -lectum	neglect	neglect
negotium, -i, n.	business, trouble	negotiate
nemo (*nullius*) (acc. *neminem*) m. or f.	nobody	

nemus, nemoris, n.	wood, grove of trees	
nequeo, -quire, -quivi, -quitum	be unable	
nequiquam	in vain	
niger, -gra, -grum	black, dark	
nihil, nil	nothing	nil
nimbus, -i, m.	cloud, storm-cloud	
{ *nimis*	too much	
nimium	too much	
nimius, -a, -um	excessive	
niteo, nitere	shine, be bright	
nitor, niti, nixus (or *nisus*) (+abl.)	rely on, strive	
nix, nivis, f.	snow	
{ *no* (1)	swim	
nato (1)	swim	
nobilis, -is, -e	noble	noble
noceo (2) (+dat.)	hurt, harm	obnoxious
nolo, nolle, nolui	be unwilling	
nomen, -minis, n.	name	nominal
{ *non*	not	non-stop
nonne	surely	
nondum	not yet	
{ *nos* (*nostrum* or *nostri*)	we	
noster, -tra, -trum	our	
{ *nosco, noscere, novi, notum*	learn, get to know	notice
novi (perfect of *nosco*)	know	
notus, -a, -um	known	notable
novus, -a, -um	new	novelty
nox, noctis, f.	night	nocturnal
nubes, nubis, f.	cloud	

nubo, nubere, nupsi, nuptum (+dat.)	marry	**nuptial**
{ *nudo* (1)	strip	
{ *nudus, -a, -um*	naked, unarmed	**nude**
{ *nullus, -a, -um*	none	**nullify**
{ *nonnullus, -a, -um*	some	
numen, -minis, n.	god, divine power	
{ *numero* (1)	count, reckon	**enumerate**
{ *numerus, -i,* m.	number	**numeral**
nunquam	never	
{ *nuntio* (1)	announce	**pronounce**
{ *nuntius, -i,* m.	messenger, news	
nuper	lately, recently	
nusquam	nowhere	

O

obliviscor, -isci, oblitus (+gen.)	forget	**oblivious**
obses, obsidis, m. or f.	hostage	
obsideo, -sidere, -sedi, -sessum	besiege	
obtineo, -tinere, -tinui, -tentum	occupy, hold on to	**obtain**
obviam eo, ire, ivi (or *ii*), *itum* (+dat.)	meet, come across	
occasio, -ionis, f.	right time, opportunity	**occasion**
occido, -cidere, -cidi, -casum	fall down, die	
occido, -cidere, -cidi, -cisum	kill	
occulo, -culere, -cului, -cultum	hide	**occult**
occupo (1)	seize	**occupy**

oculus, -i, m.	eye	oculist
odi (fut. *odero:* past *oderam*)	hate	
odium, -i, n.	hatred	odious
officium, -i, n.	duty, job	official
olim	formerly, in the past	
omen, ominis, n.	omen, sign	ominous
omnis, -is, -e	all, every	omnipotent
omnino	altogether, entirely	
onus, oneris, n.	burden	
onerosus, -a, -um	burdensome, heavy	onerous
onerarius, -a, -um	cargo-carrying	
opem, -is, f.	help	
opes, -um, f. pl.	wealth, resources	
opulentus, -a, -um	rich	opulent
operio, -rire, -rui, -rtum	cover	
opinor (1)	think, believe	
opinio, opinionis, f.	belief	opinion
oportet, -tere, -tuit	it is right	
oppidum, -i, n.	town	
oppidani, -orum, m. pl.	townsmen, citizens	
opportunus, -a, -um	suitable, at the right time	opportune
opprimo, -primere, -pressi, -pressum	crush, overwhelm	oppress
oppugno (1)	assault, attack	
opto (1)	choose, wish	option
opus, operis, n.	task, piece of work	operate
opus est (+abl)	there is a need of	
opera, -ae, f.	care, trouble	
ōra, -ae, f.	coast, shore	

orbis, -is, m.	circle, world	orbit
ordo, ordinis, m.	order, rank	ordinal
{ *orior, oriri, ortus*	arise	
{ *oriens (orientis)*	east	orient
orno (1)	adorn, decorate	ornament
{ *os, oris*, n.	mouth, face	oral
{ *ostendo, -tendere, -tendi, -tentum*	show	ostensible
{ *ostento* (1)	show	ostentatious
{ *oro* (1)	pray, beg, ask	adore
{ *orator, -oris*, m.	speaker	orator
{ *oratio, -ionis*, f.	speech	oration
os, ossis, n.	bone	ossify
otium, -i, n.	leisure, peace	
ovis, -is, f.	sheep	

P

{ *pabulor* (1)	forage, seek for food	
{ *pabulum, -i*, n.	fodder, food	
{ *paco* (1)	subdue, pacify	pacific
{ *pax, pacis*, f.	peace	
paene	almost	peninsula
paenitet, -ere, -uit	it causes repentance	penitence
palus, paludis, f.	marsh	
pando, pandere, pandi, passum	spread out, extend (trans.)	expanse
panis, -is, m.	bread	
{ *par (paris)*	equal, like	on a par with
{ *pariter*	equally, similarly	
parco, parcere, peperci, parsum (+dat.)	spare	

pāreo (2) (+ dat.)	obey	
părio, parĕre, peperi, partum	produce, get	parent
păro (1)	prepare, get	prepare
pars, partis, f.	part	part
parvus, -a, -um	small	
passus, -us, m.	step, pace	passage
pateo, patere, patui	lie open, be clear	patent
pater, patris, m.	father	paternal
patria, -ae, f.	fatherland, country	patriot
patrius, -a, -um	ancestral, hereditary	
patior, pati, passus	endure, allow	passion
pauci, -ae, -a	few	
paulum	a little, somewhat	
paulo	a little, somewhat	
paulatim	gradually	
paveo, pavere, pavi	fear	
pavor, -oris, m.	terror	
pecco (1)	sin, make a mistake	
pectus, -toris, n.	breast, heart	pectoral
pecunia, -ae, f.	money	pecuniary
pecus, pecudis, f.	animal, one of a herd	
pecus, pecoris, n.	cattle, herd	
pello, pellere, pepuli, pulsum	drive, rout	repulse
penates, -tium, m. pl.	home, household gods	
pendeo, pendēre, pependi	hang, be suspended (intrans.)	pending
pendo, pendĕre, pependi, pensum	suspend, ponder, value (trans.)	suspense

perdo, perdere, perdidi, perditum	lose, destroy, ruin	**perdition**
pereo, -ire, -ii, -itum	perish	**perish**
pergo, pergere, perrexi, perrectum	proceed, continue	
periculum, -i, n.	danger	
periculosus, -a, -um	dangerous	
peritus, -a, -um (+gen.)	skilled	
permitto, -mittere, -misi, -missum	entrust, allow	**permit**
pertineo, -tinere, -tinui	belong to, have to do with	**pertain**
pervenio, -venire, -veni, -ventum	arrive	
pes, pedis, m.	foot	**pedal**
pedes, peditis, m.	foot-soldier	
peditatus, -us, m.	infantry	
pedester, -tris, -tre	on foot	**pedestrian**
peto, petere, petivi (or *petii*), *petitum*	seek, ask, aim at	**petition**
piger, -gra, -grum	slow, lazy	
pilum, -i, n.	javelin	
piscis, -is, m.	fish	
pius, -a, -um	dutiful, loyal	**pious**
pietas, -atis, f.	sense of duty	**piety**
plăceo, placere, placui, placitum (+dat.)	please	
plăcidus, -a, -um	quiet, peaceful	**placid**
plāco (1)	reconcile, pacify	**placate**
planus, -a, -um	level	**plain**
plebs, plebis, f.	common people	**plebeian**
plenus, -a, -um (+gen.)	full	**plenty**

{ *plerique, -aeque, -aque*	most, very many	
{ *plerumque*	mostly, commonly	
pluit, pluere, pluit	it rains	
{ *poena, -ae*, f.	punishment	penalty
{ *punio* (4)	punish	punish
polliceor (2)	promise	
pondus, ponderis, n.	weight	ponderous
pono, ponere, posui, positum	place, lay aside	position
pons, pontis, m.	bridge	pontoon
pontus, -i, m.	sea	Hellespont
populus, -i, m.	a people, folk	populace
populor (1)	ravage, devastate	
porro	onwards, farther	
porta, -ae, f.	gate	portal
porto (1)	carry	porter
portus, -us, m.	harbour	port
posco, poscere, poposci	demand, ask	
possideo, -sidere, -sedi, -sessum	possess	possess
{ *possum, posse, potui*	be able	possible
{ *potestas, -atis*, f.	power	potent
⎡ *post*	after (preposition)	
│ *postea*	afterwards (adverb)	
⎨ *postquam*	after (conjunction)	
│ *posterior (posterioris)*	later, next	posterity
⎣ *postremus, -a, -um*	latest, last	
postulo (1)	demand	
potior, potiri, potitus (+ gen. or abl.)	obtain, gain	
potius	rather, preferably	
praebeo (2)	offer, show, present	

praeceps (praecipitis)	headlong, straight down	precipice
praecipito (1)	throw down, rush down	precipitate
praeda, -ae, f.	plunder, prey	prey
praemium, -i, n.	reward	premium
praesertim	especially	
praesidium, -i, n.	protection, garrison	preside
praesto, -stare, -stiti, -stitum	show, excel, perform	
praeterea	besides	
praetor, -oris, m.	praetor, president	
precor (1)	pray, beg	pray
preces, -um, f. pl.	prayers	
premo, premere, pressi, pressum	press, urge	press
pretium, -i, n.	price	precious
princeps, principis, m.	chief, leader	prince
prior (prioris)	former, previous	priority
prius	previously	
priusquam	before	
primus, -a, -um	first	prime
pristinus, -a, -um	former, ancient	
priscus, -a, -um	former, ancient	
probrum, -i, n.	disgrace, shame	
probrosus, -a, -um	disgraceful, shameful	
probus, -a, -um	good, virtuous	
probo (1)	test, approve	prove
procul	far away	
prodo, -dere, -didi, -ditum	relate, betray	
proelium, -i, n.	battle	
proficiscor, -ficisci, -fectus	set out, start off	
progredior, -gredi, -gressus	advance	progress
prohibeo (2)	prevent	prohibit

promo, promere, prompsi, promptum	bring out, produce	
promptus, -a, -um	ready	prompt
prope	near (preposition)	
propior (propioris)	nearer	
proximus, -a, -um	nearest, next	approximate
propero (1)	hasten, hurry	
prosum, prodesse, profui (+dat.)	be useful, help	
protinus	at once	
provideo, -videre, -vidi, -visum	foresee, provide for	provision
provincia, -ae, f.	province	province
prudens (prudentis)	wise, cautious	prudent
publicus, -a, -um	public	public
pudet, pudere, puduit	it causes shame	
puer, pueri, m.	boy	puerile
puella, -ae, f.	girl	
pugno (1)	fight	pugnacious
pugna, -ae, f.	fight	
pulcher, -chra, -chrum	beautiful	
pulvis, -veris, m.	dust	pulverize
puppis, -is, f.	ship, stern of a ship	
puto (1)	think	compute

Q

quaero, quaerere, quaesivi, quaesitum	seek, get, ask	
quaestor, -oris, m.	quaestor, finance officer	
quaestus, -us, m.	gain, profit	
quaestio, -ionis, f.	inquiry, law-court	question

qualis, -is, -e	of what kind	quality
quam	how, than	
quando	when	
quantus, -a, -um	how great	quantity
-que	and	
queror, queri, questus	complain	

qui, quae, quod	who, which	
quicumque, quaecumque, quodcumque	whoever, whatever	
quivis, quaevis, quodvis	anyone	
quilibet, quaelibet, quodlibet	anyone	
quidam, quaedam, quoddam	a certain person	

quia	because	
quidem	indeed, admittedly	
quies, quietis, f.	rest, calm	quiet

quis, quis, quid	who, what	
quis, qua, quid	anyone, anything	
quisquam, quaequam, quicquam	anyone, anything	
quisque, quaeque, quodque	each	
quisquis, quicquid	whoever, whatever	

quomodo	how, in what way	
quondam	formerly, in the past	
quoniam	since	
quoque	also	

quot	how many	quota
quotiens	how many times	quotient

R

ramus, -i, m.	branch of a tree

rapio, rapere, rapui, raptum	seize	rape
rapax (rapacis)	greedy, rapacious	rapacious
rapidus, -a, -um	swift	rapid
ratis, -is, f.	boat	
recens (recentis)	fresh	recent
recipio, -cipere, -cepi, -ceptum	take back	receipt
se recipere	retreat	
recuso (1)	refuse	
reddo, -ddere, -ddidi, -dditum	restore, give	render
redeo, redire, redii (or *-ivi*), *reditum*	go back, return (intrans.)	
reditus, -us, m.	return	
refert, referre, rettulit (meā, tuā, etc.)	it concerns, it profits	
rĕgo, regere, rexi, rectum	keep straight, rule	rector
rectus, -a, -um	straight, right	rectitude
rex, rēgis, m.	king	regal
regina, -ae, f.	queen	
regnum, -i, n.	kingdom	
regius, -a, -um	royal	
religio, -ionis, f.	religion	religion
relinquo, -linquere, -liqui, -lictum	leave (trans.)	relic
reliquus, -a, -um	remaining, the rest	
remus, -i, m.	oar	
renovo (1)	repair, renew	renovate
reor, reri, ratus	think	reason
ratio, -ionis, f.	reason, plan, method	rational
repentinus, -a, -um	sudden	

reperio, -ire, repperi, repertum	find	
requies, -ietis, f.	rest	requiem
res, rei, f.	thing, affair, event	real
res publica, rei publicae, f.	state, commonwealth	republic
resisto, -sistere, -stiti (+dat.)	resist	resist
respondeo, -ere, -spondi, -sponsum	reply, answer	response
restituo, -tuere, -tui, -tutum	restore	restitution
reus, -i, m.	accused person	
rideo, ridere, risi, risum	laugh	ridicule
ripa, -ae, f.	bank of a river	
robur, roboris, n.	strength	robust
rogo (1)	ask	interrogate
rota, -ae, f.	wheel	rotate
ruber, -bra, -brum	red	ruby
rudis, -is, -e	crude, clumsy	rude
rumpo, rumpere, rupi, ruptum	break (trans.)	erupt
ruo, ruere, rui, rutum	rush, fall	
ruina, -ae, f.	ruin, fall	ruin
rursus	again	
rus, ruris, n.	countryside	rural
rusticus, -a, -um	of the country	rustic

S

sacer, -cra, -crum	sacred	sacred
sacerdos, -dotis, m. or f.	priest, priestess	
saepe	often	
saevus, -a, -um	cruel	savage

{ *sagitta, -ae*, f.	arrow	
{ *sagittarius, -i*, m.	archer	
{ *salio, salire, salui, saltum*	leap, dance	
{ *salto* (1)	dance	
saltus, -us, m.	pasture-land, valley	
{ *salus, salutis*, f.	safety	
{ *salvo* (1)	save	salvation
{ *salvus, -a, -um*	safe	
sanguis, -guinis, m.	blood	
{ *sano* (1)	cure	sanatorium
{ *sanus, -a, -um*	healthy	sane
{ *satis*	enough	
{ *satisfacio, -facere, -feci,*	satisfy	satisfaction
{ *-factum* (+dat.)		
saxum, -i, n.	rock, stone	
{ *scelus, sceleris*, n.	crime	
{ *sceleratus, -a, -um*	criminal	
{ *scio, scire, scivi, scitum*	know	
{ *scientia, -ae*, f.	knowledge	science
scopulus, -i, m.	rock, crag	
scribo, scribere, scripsi,	write	scripture
scriptum		
scutum, -i, n.	shield	
{ *se (sui)*	himself, herself, itself, themselves	suicide
{ *suus, -a, -um*	his, hers, its, theirs	
seco, secare, secui, sectum	cut	section
secundus, -a, -um	second, favourable	
securus, -a, -um	free from care, serene	secure
sed	but	

sedeo, sedere, sedi, sessum	sit, wait, sink	session
sedes, sedis, f.	seat, residence, place	
sedo (1)	settle, calm, stop	sedate
seges, segetis, f.	growing corn	
segnis, -is, -e	sluggish, lazy	
semper	always	
senex, senis, m.	old man	senile
senior, -ius	old man, older	senior
senator, -oris, m.	senator	
senatus, -us, m.	senate	
sentio, sentire, sensi, sensum	perceive, judge	sense
sententia, -ae, f.	opinion, belief	sentence
sequor, sequi, secutus	follow	consequence
sero, serere, serui, sertum	join, put together	series
sero, serere, sevi, satum	sow	seed
servio, -vire, -vii, -vitum (+ dat.)	serve, be a slave	serve
servus, -i, m.	slave	serf
servitus, utis, f.	slavery	servitude
servo (1)	save, keep, preserve	preserve
severus, -a, -um	harsh, strict	severe
sic	thus, so	
siccus, -a, -um	dry	
sidus, sideris, n.	star, constellation	
signum, -i, n.	sign, battle-flag	sign
sileo, silere, silui	be silent	silent
silentium, -i, n.	silence	
silva, -ae, f.	wood, forest	
similis, -is, -e (+gen.)	like	similar
simul	at the same time	simultaneous
simul ac	as soon as	

simulo (1)	pretend	simulate
sinister, -tra, -trum *sinistra* (*manu*)	on the left on the left (hand)	sinister
sino, sinere, sivi, situm	allow, permit	
sinus, -us, m.	fold, breast, lap, bay	sinuous
sisto, sistere, stiti, statum	place, stand, stop	consistent
sive . . . sive *seu . . . seu*	whether . . . or : if . . . or if	
socius, -i, m.	friend, ally	society
sodalis, -is, m. or f.	friend, comrade	
sōl, sōlis, m.	sun	solar
sŏleo, solere, solitus	be accustomed	obsolete
sollers (*sollertis*) *sollertia, -ae*, f.	cunning cunning	
sollicito (1) *sollicitus, -a, -um* *sollicitudo, -dinis*, f.	rouse, urge, disturb disturbed anxiety, care	solicit solicitude
solor (1)	comfort	console
sŏlum, -i, n.	soil, ground	
sōlus, -a, -um *sōlum*	alone, only only	sole
solvo, solvere, solvi, *solutum*	set free, release	solve
somnus, -i, m. *somnium, -i*, n.	sleep dream	insomnia
sono, sonare, sonui, *sonitum* *sonus, -i*, m. *sonitus, -us*, m.	make a noise noise, sound noise, sound	sonorous
sopor, soporis, m.	sleep	soporific

soror, sororis, f.	sister	
sors, sortis, f.	chance, lot, fate	sorcerer
spatium, -i, n.	space, interval	space
specto (1)	look at	perspective
species, -iei, f.	appearance	species
spectaculum, -i, n.	sight, spectacle	spectacle
sperno, spernere, sprevi, spretum	despise	spurn
spero (1)	hope	despair
spes, spei, f.	hope	
sponte	of one's own accord	spontaneous
statim	immediately	
statuo, -uere, -ui, -utum	decide, establish	statute
sterno, sternere, stravi, stratum	lay flat	stratum
stipendium, -i, n.	pay, military service	stipend
sto, stare, steti, statum	stand	constant
statio, -ionis, f.	position, outpost	station
strepo, -pere, -pui	make a noise	
strepitus, -us, m.	noise	
stringo, -ingere, -inxi, -ictum	draw a sword, bind, touch	strict
studeo, studere, studui (+ dat.)	be keen on, side with	study
studium, -i, n.	enthusiasm, eagerness	
stultus, -a, -um	foolish	stultify
subeo, -ire, -ii or *-ivi, -itum*	approach, undergo	
subitus, -a, -um	sudden	
subito	suddenly	
subsidium, -i, n.	help, reserve troops	subsidy

subvenio, -venire, -veni, -ventum (+dat.)	come to help	
succurro, -currere, -curri, -cursum (+dat.)	come to help	succour
sum, esse, fui	be	essence
sumo, sumere, sumpsi, sumptum	take, consume	presume
{ *superbus, -a, -um*	proud	superb
{ *superbia, -ae,* f.	pride	
{ *supersum, -esse, -fui*	survive	
{ *superstes (superstitis)*	surviving	
{ *supplex, supplicis,* m.	suppliant, one who asks	
{ *supplico* (1) (+dat.)	beg, implore	supplication
supplicium, -i, n.	punishment, torture	
{ *supra*	above	
{ *superior (superioris)*	higher	superior
{ *supremus, -a, -um* or *summus, -a, -um*	highest, the top of	supreme
{ *superi, -orum,* m. pl.	the gods in heaven	
surgo, surgere, surrexi, surrectum	rise	resurrection
suscipio, -cipere, -cepi, -ceptum	undertake	
suspicor (1)	suspect	suspect
sustineo, -tinere, -tinui, -tentum	support, withstand	sustain

T

{ *taceo, tacere, tacui, tacitum*	be silent	
{ *tacitus, -a, -um*	silent, quiet	taciturn
{ *taedet, -dere, -duit*	it causes boredom	
{ *taedium, -i,* n.	weariness, boredom	tedious

talis, -is, -e	such	retaliate
tam	so	
tamen	but, however, yet	
tandem	at last, finally	
tango, tangere, tetigi, tactum	touch	contact
tanquam	as if	
{ *tantus, -a, -um*	so great	tantamount
{ *tantum*	only	
tardus, -a, -um	slow	tardy
{ *tego, tegere, texi, tectum*	cover	protect
{ *tectum, -i,* n.	house, building	architect
tellus, telluris, f.	earth, ground	
telum, -i, n.	weapon, javelin	
temere	rashly	temerity
templum, -i, n.	temple	temple
tempto (1)	try	attempt
{ *tempus, temporis,* n.	time	temporary
{ *tempestas, -atis,* f.	time, weather, storm	tempest
tenebrae, -arum, f. pl.	darkness, shadows	
teneo, tenere, tenui, tentum	hold, have	tenant
tener, tenera, tenerum	tender, delicate	tender
tergum, -i, n.	back, rear	
terra, -ae, f.	earth, land	terrain
{ *terreo* (2)	frighten	terrify
{ *terror, -oris,* m.	fear	terror
{ *testis, -is,* m. or f.	witness	testify
{ *testor* (1)	witness	testament
{ *timeo* (2)	fear	timid
{ *timor, -oris,* m.	fear	

tollo, tollere, sustuli, sublatum	raise, remove	
torqueo, -ere, torsi, tortum	twist, throw, torture	torture
tormentum, -i, n.	artillery	
tot	so many	
totiens	so often	
totus, -a, -um	all, whole	total
trado, -dere, -didi, -ditum	hand over, hand down (trans.)	tradition
traho, -ere, traxi, tractum	drag, pull	tractor
trepido (1)	be agitated, fear	trepidation
trepidus, -a, -um	anxious	intrepid
tribus, -us, f.	tribe	tribe
tribuo, -uere, -ui, -utum	pay, give, assign	tribute
tristis, -is, -e	sad, grim	
triumphus, -i, m.	triumph	triumph
trucido (1)	slaughter	
tu (tui)	you	
tuus, -a, -um	yours	
tueor, tueri, tuitus	watch, protect	institution
tutus, -a, -um	safe	tutor
tum	then	
tunc	then	
tumultus, -us, m.	confusion, war	tumult
tumulus, -i, m.	mound, small hill	tumulus
turba, -ae, f.	crowd, mob	
turbo (1)	confuse, disturb	disturb
turma, -ae, f.	troop, squadron	
turpis, -is, -e	disgraceful	turpitude
turris, -is, f.	tower	turret

U

{ *ubi*	where	
ubique	everywhere	ubiquitous
ulciscor, ulcisci, ultus	avenge	
ullus, -a, -um	any	
{ *ultra*	beyond	ultra-violet
ulterior (ulterioris)	further away	ulterior
ultimus, -a, -um	furthest, last	ultimate
ultro	of one's own accord	
{ *umbra, -ae,* f.	shade, shadow, ghost	umbrella
umbrosus, -a, -um	shady	
unda, -ae, f.	wave, water	undulate
{ *unde*	from where	
undique	from all sides	
universus, -a, -um	universal, all	universe
unquam	ever	
{ *unus, -a, -um*	one, single	unit
una	together	
urbs, urbis, f.	city	urban
urgeo, urgere, ursi	press, urge	urgent
uro, urere, ussi, ustum	burn (trans.)	combustion
usque	continuously	
ut, ŭtī	so that, in order that, when, as, how	
{ *uter, utra, utrum*	which (of two things)	
uterque, -traque, -trumque	each (of two things), both	
utrimque	on both sides	
{ *ūtor, ūti, ūsus* (+abl.)	use	use
ŭsus, -us, m.	use, practice, experience	
uxor, -oris, f.	wife	

V

vaco (1) (+dat.)	be free, have leisure	vacant
vacuus, -a, -um	empty	vacuum
vado, vadere, vasi, vasum	go	invade
vadum, -i, n.	ford, crossing	
vagor (1)	wander	vague
valeo (2)	be strong	prevalent
vale!	goodbye!	
validus, -a, -um	strong	valid
vallis, -is, f.	valley	valley
vallum, -i, n.	rampart	
varius, -a, -um	varied, different	variety
vasto (1)	ravage, devastate	devastate
vastus, -a, -um	huge	vast
vates, -is, m. or f.	prophet, poet	Vatican
vel	or	
-ve	or	
veho, vehere, vexi, vectum	carry	vehicle
vello, vellere, vulsi, vulsum	tear, pull away	convulsion
velut	as, just as	
vendo, -dere, -didi, -ditum	sell	vendor
veneror (1)	worship, respect	venerate
venia, -ae, f.	pardon, mercy	venial
venio, venire, veni, ventum	come	event
ventus, -i, m.	wind	ventilate
ver, veris, n.	springtime	
verbum, -i, n.	word	verbal
vereor (2)	fear	reverent
vertex, -ticis, f.	whirl, head, top	vertical
verto, vertere, verti, versum	turn (trans.)	avert

verus, -a, -um	true	verify
veritas, -atis, f.	truth	veritable
vero	but, indeed	
vesper, -peris, m.	evening	vespers
vestigium, -i, n.	trace, footprint	vestige
vestis, -is, f.	clothes	vestments
vestio (4)	clothe	invest
veto, vetare, vetui, vetitum	forbid, order not to	veto
vetus (veteris)	old	veteran
via, -ae, f.	road, way	viaduct
vicus, -i, m.	village	
vicinus, -a, -um	near-by, neighbouring	vicinity
video, videre, vidi, visum	see	vision
visus, -us, m.	glance, vision	visible
vigilia, -ae, f.	guard, watch	vigilant
vigilo (1)	watch	
vincio, vincire, vinxi, vinctum	bind, tie up	
vinculum, -i, n.	chain, bond	
vinco, vincere, vici, victum	conquer, win	convince
victor, -oris, m.	conqueror	victor
victoria, -ae, f.	victory	victory
vir, viri, m.	man, hero	virile
virtus, virtutis, f.	courage, virtue	virtue
virgo, virginis, f.	girl	virgin
viridis, -is, -e	green	
vis, f. (plural *vires*)	strength, force	
vita, -ae, f.	life	vital
vivo, vivere, vixi, victum	live	revive
vivus, -a, -um	alive	vivacious

vĭtium, -i, n.	fault, defect	vice
vīto (1)	avoid	
vix	hardly, scarcely	
{ *vŏco* (1)	call	vocation
{ *vox, vōcis,* f.	voice	vocal
{ *volo, velle, volui*	want, wish	
{ *voluntas, -atis,* f.	wish, will	voluntary
voluptas, -atis, f.	pleasure	voluptuous
volvo, volvere, volvi, volutum	roll (trans.)	revolve
{ *vos (vestrum* or *vestri)*	you	
{ *vester, -tra, -trum*	your	
votum, -i, n.	wish, vow, prayer	vote
{ *vulnero* (1)	wound	vulnerable
{ *vulnus, -neris,* n.	wound	
vultus, -us, m.	face, appearance.	

PREPOSITIONS AND PREFIXES

1. The following is a full list of Latin prepositions:

A. TAKING THE ACCUSATIVE

ad	to, towards	*inter*	between, among
adversus	towards, against	*intra*	within
ante	before	*iuxta*	next to, beside
apud	at, near, among	*ob*	on account of
circum	around, about (of things)	*penes*	in the power of
		per	through, by means of
circa	about (of time or numbers)	*pone*	behind
		post	after, behind
circiter	about (of time or numbers)	*praeter*	beside, past, along
		prope	near
cis	on this side of	*propter*	on account of
citra	on this side of	*secundum*	along, according to
clam	unknown to, in secret	*supra*	above
contra	against	*trans*	across
erga	towards (of feelings)	*ultra*	beyond
extra	outside	*versus*	towards
infra	below		

B. TAKING THE ABLATIVE

a, ab, abs	by, from	*palam*	in sight of, openly
absque	without	*prae*	before, in front of
coram	in the presence of	*pro*	on behalf of, for
cum	with	*sine*	without
de	down from, concerning	*tenus*	as far as
ex, e	out of		

53

C. Taking the Accusative (when movement over space or time is
   involved) and Ablative (when rest at a point of space or time is
   involved)

in	into, against, on, in	*super*	over, upon
sub	up to, under	*subter*	under

2. The following is a list of those prepositions and prefixes used in compound words:

a, ab, abs, au-	away, from	(*absum, abrumpo, aufero*)	absent
ad, ac-, af-, al-, etc.	to, towards	(*accipio, affero, adeo, alligo*)	accept
ante	before	(*antecedo, antepono*)	antecedent
circum	around	(*circumsto, circumfero*)	circumference
cum, con-, co- etc.	together, with	(*convoco, colligo, consto*)	collect
de	down	(*descendo, decurro*)	descend
dis-, di-	away, apart	(*discedo, disrumpo*)	disrupt
e, ex, ef-, etc.	out	(*exeo, effero, erumpo*)	erupt
in	into, not	(*ineo, innocens*)	intercept
inter	between, among	(*intercludo, intercipio*)	innocent
intro-	inside	(*introeo, introduco*)	introduce
ob	in the way of	(*obstruo, obsum*)	obstacle
per	through, thoroughly	(*perrumpo, permaneo*)	permanent
post	after	(*posthabeo, postpono*)	postpone
prae	before, in charge of	(*praevenio, praesum*)	prevent
praeter	past, along	(*praetereo, praetermitto*)	
pro	forward	(*procedo, procurro*)	proceed
re-, red-	back, again	(*refero, retineo*)	retain
se-	apart, separate	(*separo, secerno*)	separate
sub, suc-, suf-, etc.	up to, under	(*subsideo, succurro*)	subside
subter	under	(*subterlabor, subterfluo*)	subterfuge
trans	across, through	(*transfero, transeo*)	transfer

NUMBERS

1	unus, -a, -um	1st	primus,	-a,	-um,	once	semel
2	duo (gen. duorum)	2nd	secundus		,,	twice	bis
3	tres, tres, tria	3rd	tertius		,,	3 times	ter
4	quattuor	4th	quartus		,,	4 times	quater
5	quinque	5th	quintus		,,	5 times	quinquiens
6	sex	6th	sextus		,,	6 times	sexiens
7	septem	7th	septimus		,,	7 times	septiens
8	octo	8th	octavus		,,	8 times	octiens
9	novem	9th	nonus		,,	9 times	noviens
10	decem	10th	decimus		,,	10 times	deciens
11	undecim	20th	vicensimus		,,	20 times	viciens
12	duodecim	100th	centensimus		,,	100 times	centiens
13	tredecim	1000th	millensimus		,,	1000 times	milliens

14 quattuordecim
15 quindecim
16 sedecim
17 septendecim
18 duodeviginti
19 undeviginti
20 viginti
30 triginta
40 quadraginta
50 quinquaginta
60 sexaginta
70 septuaginta
80 octoginta
90 nonaginta
100 centum
200 ducenti, -ae, -a
300 trecenti, -ae, -a
400 quadringenti, -ae, -a
500 quingenti, -ae, -a
600 sescenti, -ae, -a
700 septingenti, -ae, -a
800 octingenti, -ae, -a
900 nongenti, -a e, -a
1000 mille
2000 duo milia (gen. milium)

CONSTRUCTIONS

Name	Use	Construction	Examples and Notes
DIRECT QUESTIONS	For all questions in English ending with a question mark.	Question word + indic. *nonne* = surely . . . : *num* = surely not . . . : *-ne* asks an open question: *an* = or: *annon* = or not	Who are you? = *Quis es?* Is he Caesar? *Est -ne Caesar?* How does he do it? = *Quomodo facit?*
DIRECT COMMANDS	For English imperative e.g. ' stay here ', ' don't go away ', etc.	Imperative. If a neg. comd., *noli* + infin.	Do this = *fac hoc*. Don't go = *noli ire*.
WISHES	For English ' would that ', ' may you be ', etc.	*Utinam* + Pres. time: imp. subj. Past time: plup. subj. Fut. time: pres. subj.	May you be happy! = *Utinam sis felix*. Would that he were here now! = *utinam nunc adesset*.
INDIRECT STATEMENT	For ' he said that ', ' I hope to ', ' We think that ' ' Promise to ', etc.	Acc. and infin. (acc. is always needed for a person, e.g. ' *me* ' in the example).	I hope to come = *spero me venturum esse*. He said that he had done it = *dixit se id fecisse*.
INDIRECT COMMAND	For ' persuading to ', ' advising to ', asking to ' and all verbs of getting someone to do something.	*Ut* or *ne* + subj. (this translates ' to ' and ' not to ' in the English).	Persuade him to go = *Suade ei ut eat*. BUT N.B. *JUBEO* (= ' order ' or ' tell ') TAKES INFIN.
INDIRECT QUESTION	Always has a question word, but no question mark.	Question word + subj. (fut. subj. when needed) whether = *num*: whether . . . or . . . = *utrum . . . an . . .*: whether . . . or not = *utrum . . . necne*.	I know what it is = *scio quid sit*. I asked what he would do = *rogavi quid facturus esset*.

NAME	USE	CONSTRUCTION	EXAMPLES AND NOTES
FINAL (Purpose)	Always means 'in order to ', or ' with the purpose of '.	*Ut* or *ne* +subj. (' So that no one ' =*ne quis*, etc., i.e. any neg. needs a ' *ne* '.) N.B. never write ' *et ne* ': use ' *neve* '.)	He went to see = *Ivit ut videret.* He works in order that he may never be beaten = *laborat ne unquam caedatur.*
CONSECUTIVE (Result)	Always expresses the *result*: usually a word like ' so ', ' so many ', in the main sentence.	*Ut* or *ut non* +subj. (' so that no one ' =*ut nemo*, etc., i.e. you keep the ' *ut* ' always).	There are so many ships that the harbour cannot be seen = *tot naves sunt ut portus non videri possit.*
CONDITIONAL	To translate ' if ' or ' unless ' (=*si* or *nisi*).	(1) If there is a ' would ' or ' should ', both parts go in subj. (2) If not, both indic. *With wd. or shd.* Pres. time = 2 imp. subj. Past time = 2 plup. subj. Fut. time = 2 pres. subj. *Without wd. or shd.* Pres. time = 2 pres. ind. Past time = 2 past ind. Fut. time = 2 fut. ind.	If you were here now, you would see me = *si nunc adesses me videres.* If you had done this, you would have been beaten = *si hoc fecisses, caesus esses.* If you go tomorrow, you will see me = *si cras ibis me videbis.*
CAUSAL	'Because', or 'on the grounds that ' (any word giving a reason	*Quod* +indic. if it means ' because in fact ': +subj. if it means ' because (as they thought)' or anything not certainly a fact.	He was unjustly killed, on the grounds that he was an enemy = *inuste necatus est quod esset hostis.* He went there because he wanted to = *ivit eo quod voluit ire.*
CONCESSIVE	' Although ', ' even though ' (anything conceding a point).	If clause states a fact, *quamquam* +indic. If not, *quamvis* +subj.	Although it is cold, I shall go out = *quamquam est frigidum, exibo.* Even though he may be wise, I don't trust him = *quamvis sit sapiens, non ei confido.*

NAME	USE	CONSTRUCTION	EXAMPLES AND NOTES
COMPARATIVE	'As', 'as if', 'As though'	If a fact, *ut* or *sicut* + indic. (for English ' as '): if not. *quasi* + subj. (for English ' as if ').	He defeated me today as he always does = *vicit me hodie ut semper facit*. He spoke Latin well, as if he were a Roman = *Latinam linguam bene est locutus, quasi Romanus esset*.
PROVISO	' Provided that ' or ' as long as '	*Dum* + subj.	Let them hate, provided that they fear = *oderint dum metuant*. I will go as long as I am allowed to return = *ibo, dum liceat mihi redire*.
VERBS OF FEARING	(1) fear *to* (2) fear *that*	(1) infinite (2) *Ne* or *ne non* + subj. (' *ne* ' is for English ' that ' or ' lest ').	I am afraid to go = *Timeo ire*. I fear he may be killed = *timeo ne necetur*. Caesar was afraid that he might not arrive there = *Caesar timuit ne non eo adveniret*.
TEMPORAL	All words of time	*CUM* = when: indic. if prim., subj. if historic. *DUM* = while: always + *pres.* indic. *DUM* = until: subj. *QUOTIENS* = whenever *POSTQUAM* = after *ANTEQUAM* = before *SIMUL AC* = as soon as ALL + INDIC.	When you come, you will see = *cum venies, videbis*. (N.B. future tense.) When I had done this, I slept = *Cum hoc fecissem, dormivi*. While I slept, a dream came = *dum dormio, somnium venit*. Wait until I come = *mane dum veniam*. After he had done this, he departed = *postquam hoc fecit, abiit*.
PRICE AND VALUE	Buying, valuing, selling	If a stated sum of money + ablative. If not + genitive. N.B. *aestimo* = think worth, value: *aestimor* = be worth, cost.	He sold it for three talents = *Hoc vendidit tribus talentis*. He bought it for a small price = *Hoc emit parvi*. How much is it worth? = *Quanti aestimatur?* (lit. ' at how much is it valued? ')

Name	Use	Construction	Examples and Notes
Hinder and Doubt	'Hinder from', or 'doubt that'	*IMPEDIO* = hinder: if positive, *ne* or *quominus* + subj. If negative, *quin* + subj. *DUBITO* = doubt: if positive, it is an Indirect Q: if neg., *quin* + subj.	They were hindered from going = *Impediebantur ne irent*. I do not hinder him from going = *non eum impedio quin eat*. I doubt whether he is brave = *dubito num sit fortis* There is no doubt that he is wise = *non dubium est quin sit sapiens*. N.B. *PROHIBEO* = prevent + INFIN.

SEQUENCE OF TENSES

PRIMARY: INDIC.: Pres., Perf., Fut., Fut. Perf.

SUBJ.: Pres., Perf. (Fut. for Indirect Questions only).

E.g.: I { know / have known / shall know } what he { does / has done / will do } = { scio / scivi / sciam } quid { faciat / fecerit / facturus sit }.

HISTORIC: INDIC.: Imperf., Aorist, Pluperf.

SUBJ.: Imperf., Pluperf. (Fut. for Indirect Questions only).

E.g.: I { was asking / asked / had asked } where they { were going / had gone / would go } = { rogabam / rogavi / rogaveram } quo { irent / ivissent / ituri essent }.

VERBS TAKING INFINITIVE

statuo } = decide
constituo }
iubeo = order
prohibeo = prevent
veto = forbid (order not to)
sino } = allow
patior }

possum = be able
volo = wish
incipio } = begin
coepi }
desino = cease
conor = try
audeo = dare

cogo = compel, force
malo = prefer
soleo = be accustomed to
debeo = must, have to, ought
cupio = desire
nolo = be unwilling